# TO YOU FROM YOU

### BY FARAH ALQATTAN

Rwh Publishing LLC

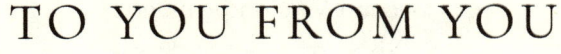

TO YOU FROM YOU

Copyright © 2023 by Farah Alqattan
www.farahalqattan.com

All rights reserved. No part of this book may be reproduced in any manner whatsoever without written permission except in the case of brief quotations embodied in critical articles and reviews.

Second Version print, 2023
ISBN: 979-8-9881785-2-1
E-BOOK ISBN: 979-8-9881785-1-4
Library of Congress Control Number: 2023939513
For permission requests, contact: Support@farahalqattan.com
Author Instagram: farahalqattanofficial
Publisher Instagram: Rwhpublishing
Edited by Mikaela Grantham

Rwh Publishing LLC produces creative content by artists who aim to uplift humanity and change lives for the better.

Words from the Author

*This book is a token of appreciation to life, from the bottom of my heart,* **thank you.**

## *Table of Contents*

To You, From You _____ Page 7
Glimmer of Hope _____ Page 8
Hidden Treasure _____ Page 9
Iris _____ Page 10
Pearl Radiance _____ Page 11
True Beauty in Numbers _____ Page 12
Silver Linings _____ Page 13
I See You, See You _____ Page 14
Great Fortitude _____ Page 15
Sweet Symphony _____ Page 16
Symphony Interconnected _____ Page 17
Simplify _____ Page 18
Guided Intuitions _____ Page 19
Voyage Architect _____ Page 20
Au Revoir _____ Page 21
Persistent Dedication _____ Page 22
Embracing Authenticity _____ Page 23
Reach the Surface _____ Page 24
Daring Vows _____ Page 25
Blessings in Disguise _____ Page 26
Delicate Craft _____ Page 27
You are Beautiful _____ Page 28

| | |
|---|---|
| Radiant Aura | Page 29 |
| Stay Gold | Page 44 |
| Serendipity | Page 30 |
| Empowered Soul | Page 32 |
| Kindred Genetics | Page 34 |
| Cultured Creations | Page 35 |
| Subjective Creations | Page 36 |
| Transformational Disciplines | Page 37 |
| Moon Walk | Page 38 |
| Here | Page 39 |
| Innocence Within You | Page 40 |
| Stay True | Page 41 |
| Butterfly Effect | Page 43 |
| Incremental Prosperity | Page 44 |
| Energy in Motion, Emotion | Page 46 |
| One in the Same | Page 47 |
| Blueprint Strategy | Page 48 |
| Beauty Marks | Page 51 |
| Humble Reassurance | Page 52 |
| Character Development | Page 54 |
| Big Picture | Page 55 |
| Lasting Impressions | Page 55 |
| Healed People, Hear People, Heal People | Page 58 |
| Love | Page 60 |
| Joys of Life | Page 61 |
| Terrain Distinction | Page 62 |
| Mi Amor | Page 63 |
| Intrinsic Design | Page 65 |
| Everlasting Union | Page 66 |
| Authenticity from Within | Page 67 |
| Distinct Determination | Page 68 |
| Uttered Nourishment | Page 69 |
| Calligraphy of the Heart | Page 70 |

Code of Honor _____ Page 71
Propelled Elevation _____ Page 72
Illuminate _____ Page 74
The Brightside _____ Page 76
Kinetic Assembly _____ Page 77
Social Medicine _____ Page 78
Speaking into Existence _____ Page 79
Heart of Gold _____ Page 80
Dancing Star _____ Page 81
Lean In _____ Page 82
Brotherly Love _____ Page 83
Steadfast _____ Page 84
Vital Vision _____ Page 86
Respectful Civilization _____ Page 87
Value of Richness _____ Page 88
Universal Welfare _____ Page 89
Bullseye _____ Page 90
Resonance _____ Page 91
Inquisitive Inquiries _____ Page 92
Structural Composition _____ Page 93
Peace Within _____ Page 94
Gratitude _____ Page 95
Harmony of Choice _____ Page 96
Compounded Momentum _____ Page 97

*Answer to You* _____ Page 98
*Neo-Cortex* _____ Page 99
*Revival* _____ Page 100
*Life* _____ Page 101
*United Nations* _____ Page 102
*Human Race* _____ Page 103
*Ripple Effect* _____ Page 104
*Principle Bound* _____ Page 105
*Nobel Duty* _____ Page 106
*Gracious Heart* _____ Page 108
*Honey Do* _____ Page 109
*Splendid* _____ Page 110
*Radiance* _____ Page 111
*Regenerative* _____ Page 112
*Dreamers Awake* _____ Page 113
*Destiny* _____ Page 114
*Cognitive Dissonance* _____ Page 115
*Savor* _____ Page 116
*Let It In* _____ Page 117
*Supernova* _____ Page 118
*Way of the World* _____ Page 119
*Happy Birthday* _____ Page 120

TO YOU FROM YOU

## To You, From You

I love you
Don't doubt you
What is in your heart will find you
Love echoes in the raindrops hitting around you
when you've felt storms

I hope you've come to care for your being
I hope you've come to understand those around
you
The signs that guide you come in all forms of
design
Symptoms and patterns

Look up at the sky and know that it all matters,
made up of matter
The moments shared in smiles and laughter,
misunderstanding and sadness,
relief and embraces
The present
Your gift
As you are to it

## Glimmer of Hope

You are strong
Resilient
When push came to shove,
you knew what your heart felt,
what you're made of

Every memory made and created in this space of
design,
through love
Even if it was not returned to you

The world experience is meant to elevate the love
song felt in hearts and souls
As you reflect back on it, you'll see it unfold

Please don't be mean
What we are meant to be is anything but that

Help
Love
Shine
Share; yourself

Whether you're a star in the movies,
the sky, or amongst the people
Your glimmer flickers
Like the twinkle in your eyes
A light

### *Hidden Treasure*

*The journey is beautiful
There are life forms all around you
Hear the echo of all that is life, surrounding you
Intuition whispers*

*You'll always find your way
You see not only in sight, but also in vision
Insight
All sense of your being
All that is internal
All that is external
All that is eternal*

*Those before us wrote these words,
helping to guide us to our truths
My sweet, it is not black or white
Open your eyes,
what do you see by your god given eyes?
Sight of sunrises and sunsets*

*You're a gem between the rocks
Cry if you must
It is okay
Water is life*

### Iris

You're made of miracles
All that you have become is extra- ordinary
Breathe this air
All the beauties of this space are shared with you
As it's within you

Enjoy nature and nurture those in it
All that surrounds you is part of it
Don't doubt it

In sharing yourself, you'll share a message
Be harmonious with your present
Cause harm to no one
Think before you act
When it is all said and done,
we leave here without wonder

Expect the unexpected
No expectations
Develop standards for the things you stand for
Enjoy the journey
In blessings you'll be surrounded
Make no mistakes, we are always forgiven
Watched over and protected

## *Pearl Radiance*

*You've wandered and wondered*
*Having faith and fear*
*All the experiences you go through are there*
*to help you get up here*
*Now*

*How you've grown to be is irreplaceable*
*You're seen and watched over*
*You've been good to yourself and those around*
*you*

*Celebrate victories*
*Celebrate life with smiles*
*You've traveled miles*

*Strive to live each day as it is not your last*
*Plant seeds*
*Not in chaos*
*But in humility*
*Express gratitude and appreciation*
*In good times and bad, you'll make it through*
*We believe in you*

## _True Beauty in Numbers_

Lay weapons down
All forms who love have been born with you,
before, and after you

The miracles of life are all that surround you
In a moment of righteousness
We're neither right or wrong
Remember the importance of what has felt right
Love darling
It does not lie
It is on the other side of all that separates us

Set aside entitlements, ego, and pride
The cause of disease is being in dis ease
You trust others every moment of every day
Strangers are your friends and family
Stitching you when you've been broken

Speak with ease
We're delicate
Humanity
Family

## <u>Silver Linings</u>

The truth of your soul echoes with you
You come and go seemingly within and out of its direction
Have no worries
Have no doubts
For all that radiates within your heartbeat comes to life
Do you hear it?

-get quiet-

Sounds louder and louder
Allow yourself to relax into it
Like the sound of existence even with all the noise surrounding it
In stillness

When you rest your head on a pillow, what comes to mind?
Is it the material of all you can find?
Face of you?
Face of someone else?
Trophies or regrets?

Reflect in a growth mindset
Progress
Lifting higher
To higher self

## *I See You, See You*

Your outlook on life affects your internal story
With a shift in perspective,
you can write a new story

Not asking to abandon or force
In a deciding moment,
you can see things different
And in turn, feel magnificent

All it ever was,
Is
Or will be
Love

This world may seem in chaos
Full of destruction, suffering, and aches
But in this moment,
reading these words is a difference you can make
Reason with peace, harmony, and understanding
Embrace the seasons with caring reason
The difference you can make starts with you

How will you use your power?
Harness dreams and visions
Bring them into the spaces of design
Home shelters

### *Great Fortitude*

*You've been met in such lows*
*You've come to learn what you're made of in the*
*triumph of wars*
*Don't look at the past in anguish*
*You're a majestic being*
*with armor invisible to many*
*Felt throughout centuries*

*Speak kindly, you're part of the design and*
*source of creation itself*
*The physical experience can be enjoyable*
*It is hard*
*It is unfair*
*It is beauty and decay*
*It takes your breath away*
*And gives it right back.*
*It reminds you of gratitude*
*It reminds of love*
*It reminds you of you,*
*who you really are,*
*and grow to trust*

*Keep going like a phoenix who inspires peace*
*Knowing the power to crawl out of buried worlds*
*Reach highs without needing to get high*
*Know that your feet never left the ground*
*Be grounded*

*Don't give up on the story*
*It is far from over*

## Sweet Symphony

*Solid*
*Fluid*
*You're composed of both*
*See the world as you know your deepest self to be*
*In the eyes of a child*

*This world in its pursuit can feel as if it drifts us*
*But it delivers us*
*It brings us closer together*

*Your focus and attention are power*
*How will you spend them?*
*Pay attention, it pays!*

*Don't put your sense of 'me' ahead of all that*
*exists before you*
*Walk side by side with those in your journey,*
*they've helped you*

*Like the collective of ants*
*Work together for one another*

*You're a Queen*
*You're a King*
*You're a Princess*
*And you're a Prince*
*All attributes of who you are, accepted*

### *<u>Interconnected</u>*

*The friction that has occurred from boxing the
self is not part of the circle of life
Accept circumstance for what they are
Radical acceptance
Know that what is external doesn't define you*

*You've come such a long way
Look at the eyes before you
As reflections of mirrors
A window to the soul*

*Those before us were given these words
The interpretation over time has been skewed
Like gossip rewritten
Lost in translation*

*But love
Love saves us
And it comes in all forms
This book, flowers blooming around you,
Smiles of friends
Linked beyond comprehension
Generations*

### <u>Simplify</u>

Calm the mind and listen to your spirit
The sound of judgment and hate is loud
But answer with love
Answer through you

-Breathe-
Do it once more
-Breathe deeply-

You belong here
Take in the great design of all that is for you
Rightfully given without control
We love you, as you are, for who you are

Don't stand still
Or stunned
Move, forward
Do your bits
Little bit at a time

Try to calm the oceans of your mind,
you're made of water

Treasure is in the eye of the beholders
The believers
It's going to be okay
Have faith

### <u>Guided Intuitions</u>

*You're so magnificent and beautiful
Like a distinguished flower in a unique garden
As you look at trees,
have you come across any that are the same
shape, size, or colors?*

*The material of the world gives you nothing,
as the love you give to yourself and those around
you.
For then you would be able to understand
all that binds us,
would not blinds us.*

Service

*The easy road is not the high road
Enjoy the journey with its highs and lows
See it all unfold like a present,
with your presence*

*Do with love
Come and go with love
This space is a home
Walk in it as you walk into your own house
Pick up your trash
Smile at your family, they're part of it*

*Earn your credentials
Aim high
For the sky*

## *Voyage Architect*

You came into this world crying
But allow yourself to feel the joy
Developed
The shelters and places bringing us together

Walk distances, sail oceans, fly over mountains
arrive at places of gatherings
ready to meet you
No matter the destination
You're always expected as accepted

Sighs of relief
Exhale of worries
Feel the power you hold
When you free your mind
How much clutter can you find?

You're constantly moving, radiating, evolving,
growing
Even on autopilot, autonomous
You're on the direction of your journey by a
compass
implemented from afar,
connected to all that is,
as it holds all that is within
True north

### *Au Revoir*

*Share these words in the silence of the mind*
*Read them out loud*
*Give away worries in the confines of those that*
*love you*
*For love is all around you*

*Sail the seas of wonder*
*This is your ship*
*Try not to crash into someone else's*
*Respect*
*Look after others*
*No man left behind*
*Is the fundamental foundation of our time*

## <u>Persistent Dedications</u>

*Challenge yourself to do things that bring health
and wellness
Appreciate presence*

*Every step taken is a direction
A destination made to be beautiful
Leaving this world better than it was found
If you doubt it
Reflect over the experience over time*

*Be thankful for every wrong turn
It has served to put you back on track
As hard as it is to adjust
Give it time, smooth sailing
Alignment
Grit gears
No worries
You're still here*

## _Embracing Authenticity_

What is the deep truth of the heart?

Is it
Patience
Trust
Humility
Laughs and smiles

If resentment and hurt find you
Do your counts
Exercise
The body
Forgiveness and grace
For love is truly on its way

Use the tools that have been created
Apologize
Give thanks even in tough times
Move on and let go
Even through the storms
Be proud of the person you're becoming
Be better, never bitter
A Sweetheart

## Reach the Surface

So, glow
Radiate
Help others find their way
Allow those who need it to find their spark in time
Respect their journey
Appreciate your own
Understand it all happens with time
Trust sweet
People are most often not where we left them

You are an adventurer
You are a survivor
You are a warrior
You are peace
You are stillness
You are human
You are brave
You are resilient

The story is far from over
At the end of your rope, tie a knot
hang in there
Floods of emotions won't hold you down
Swim
This is a life jacket

### <u>Daring Vows</u>

*You are okay*
*It will be okay*
*Feelings are temporary and will pass*
*Develop healthy routines,*
*that make things last*
*Find friends between the pages*
*Read on*
*Whether it's the Bible or Quran*
*Any form of text*

*Be as open to reading the science of intellect*
*That stems from the spirit and of design*
*It's truly a holy experience you'll come to find*

## _Blessings in Disguise_

Impressive
Extra-ordinary
What does that mean to you?
Potential
Progress
As you discover language
As it has been taught and spoken
Understand that the sum of parts together
binding to give meaning

Just like you
Oh sweet
Each experience has an affect
Everyone is trying their best

What difference can one make?
Feeling more or feeling less
In those moments
In this moment
Smile at the rest
Relax and do your bits
Little bit at a time
Patience
A virtue

## *Delicate Craft*

*Understanding power is grace*
*Recognizing the lessons and blessings,*
*is what pays*

*Do you recognize your ways?*
*Are you aware of what you're wanting?*
*What are you feeling?*
*What are you thinking?*
*Most importantly, what can you do about it?*

*Forgive or revenge*
*Love or resent*
*Walk or be dormant*
*Speak with kindness or trash*
*Life is a canvas*
*You hold the brush*
*What will you make of it?*
*See your true colors*

### *You are Beautiful*

That chatter in the mind
Make sure it is a good one
Something that would soothe a child

Why do it to yourself?
Learn through
So you can be more
As you've learned essence from those around you
Mirror neurons

The words of those who hurt you,
don't belong within you
Let it go, so it doesn't consume you
Here empowering you, rise
Not encompassed in a high
It is just a 'hi'
Meet new people
Make new friends
Our connection links us deeper than roots to the
soil of the earth

What world do you want to create?
By create
Know you've been created
And by sharing your creation
Who you really are, is the wonder
Of what makes you wonderful

## Radiant Aura

The power of influence is vast
When you walk in what identifies you,
you'll feel pride
But I challenge you to see yourself without the
labels of the world

Don't let the eyes of those who judge you,
to undress or hurt you
No one has the power to redesign you

So be strong
Be happy
Be brave
Stand tall
Stay true
You are great

Make peace with it
An offering

## *Stay Gold*

*Put yourself in someone else's shoes*
*Have you noticed that even yours have changed*
*over time*
*We grow in ways*
*We shrink in others*
*Be patient*
*Choose understanding*
*Choose silence over the words of weapon*
*Sharing yourself different in spurs of moods, attitudes, and*
*mindsets*
*How do you see others?*
*Is it worth it?*
*They too have a story*
*That comes from love and pain*
*Lives full of heartache*
*Peoples lenses are shaped by perceptions*
*As your thoughts have spiraled you up and down*
*The choices you have made*
*Offer grace*
*Love*
*For love changes and brings us back to stability*

*The gift of hands are giving hands*
*Hold yours together and those of others*
*Give the unexpected. a smile*
*Kindness*
*Even to your enemies*
*Thank them for the role they have played*

## _Serendipity_

*You are unique*
*You are different*
*But how will you use your gifts and talents?*

*You will grow to understand deeper*
*Share in realness*
*Respect and authenticity*
*See the journey through*
*Know where you are today is not where you will*
*be forever*
*It does get better*

## Empowered Soul

You are not a victim
You've been wronged
You've been harmed

Don't let words define you
For each word brings about a flood of emotions

Sadness
Pain
Hurt
Rejection

Don't let them define you

If anything defines you,
let it be the things that make you happy
Bring your will into it
The triumph of overcomings
Resiliency
Grit
For it is mind over matter
And what matters creates mindsets

So how do you talk to yourself?
What does it mean to be a victim?
Does it make you feel better?
Repeating the story and narrative
Over and over
Its over

*Give yourself compassion*
*Give yourself permission to move on*
*Give yourself love*
*Give yourself grace*

*For even those who wronged you will answer to*
*the reckoning of their ways*
*And by reckoning,*
*it is something we all will come to feel*

*So forgive*
*And grieve*
*Let it go*
*Take your time*
*Don't live in the suffering*
*Try to make something of it*
*Like this book*

*Ask yourself these important questions,*
*Did I laugh enough?*
*Did I love enough?*
*Did I make a difference?*

### *Kindred Genetics*

*Ease the mind*
*It is that easy*
*Breathe deeply*

*It might take a day, it might take you a month,*
*it might take years*
*Know time is of the essence*
*It's been on your side*

*The gift of life*
*You made it*
*Here*

*Given permission to feel*
*You've fought, cried, smiled, and laughed*
*You've been angry and angered*
*It's okay*
*Grow*
*Rejoice in this walk of life*
*In truth*
*Uphold integrity, do what is right*
*Remember words are weapons*
*Use love as a language*
*Lead with compassion*
*Empathy too*
*You and me, we, with us, it's in us*

## *Cultured Creations*

*Push and pull*
*Adventure and venture back*
*There's no race*
*It is a walk of life*

*The destination is the same for all of us*
*The journey is unique for you as it has been for*
*your parents,*
*grandparents, friends, and children*
*In the end, we feel the same*
*So see them in beauty*
*Prepare each for the emotions they'll have to face*
*As you have come to face them yourself*
*Reflect on how it has influenced*

*Remember to give thanks as the footprints you*
*leave behind*
*For what touches the heart, touches all of us*
*As you will come to find*
*Founded in the foundation of mannerisms*
*Harmonious and diligent*

### Subjective Creations

The development of your being occurred outside
of your control
Surrender your force to change the past
Allow for all that created you to work for you
Set your eye on treasure, the present
Intention

Create your dreams
Knowing that what you bring to this space is
shared in diversity

Grace, understand influence
You've been influenced
Let love guide you
The story is a compass

Morals
Values
Principles

The foundation and building blocks of humanity
Do wrong to none, especially yourself
Your body is a temple
You hold the key
The code is universal

## _Transformational Disciplines_

*These words bring truths*
*More for them does not mean less for you*
*Being mean is less of you*

*There is abundance*

*Ask of you and it shall be given*
*As you take it all in*
*Give back as you were given*

*Pay it forward*
*Pay attention*
*Step outside of selfish mindset*

*Choose to grow*
*Learn*
*Newness*
*For even that becomes familiar*
*Adaptation*
*Time is on your side*

*World full of wonders, oh so wonderful*
*Consistency, will power*
*Habits*
*A teaching*
*Hone down*
*Discipline*

### <u>Moon Walk</u>

*Life is not a popularity contest*
*For even those that rise in fame find rock bottom*
*Learning the roots of the soil beneath our feet is*
*fundamental to nature*
*No hard lesson*
*It is only love*
*At times, it can be hard*
*The movement*
*Is a revolution*
*Revelation*

*Earth spinning around in rotation*

## *Here*

*There was no mistake in creating you*
*Grow knowing your attributes*
*Influences*
*Motivations*
*Strengths*
*Weakness*
*Talents*
*Delicate and strong*

*Do what you must and utilize resources*
*They are here to help and heal you*
*Know that the biggest difference you can make*
*in feeling better starts within you*

*Choose to prioritize wellbeing*
*Go outside and play*
*Feel the sun rays*
*Drops of rain giving life*
*Universal qualities*
*Shared in quantities*

## *Innocence Within You*

*You have come a long way*
*How far is your childhood?*
*Can you tap back into it?*
*The ease and play*
*The loving attitude*
*The moment of upset turned into giggles,*
*with a tickle*

*You indeed have come so far*
*Be proud of yourself*

*Cry if you need, release the pain*
*That you were never meant to harbor*
*Laugh about it, humor is a medicine*
*And if you're numb or life seems out of control*
*Meditate in nature*
*Be surrounded in the oasis of life that has*
*nurtured humanity over time*

*Tree of life*
*Nurseries*

*Close your eyes and believe*
*Trust that it will get better*
*Believe it in your bones*
*You hold the key*
*Have faith, no fear*
*Guiding you here*

## Stay True

You've got a heart of gold
Don't look at the past in regret or guilt

You continue to treat the life around you with love
Teach by your example
Lead with the change you want to be met with
Hold it in your heart
There will be those who doubt
But they too will find and feel love as you have

It changes you
It makes you rise above
"never quit; never give up"
Keep going
Be encouraging
Be inspiring
Know it all reflects back at you
Rest as you need
The story is far from over
It only gets better from here

## *Butterfly Effect*

*Choose to stay*
*Choose family*
*For family is all around you*
*Choose kindness*

*Care about yourself*
*Choose to smile*
*Choose to figure it out*
*Choose life*
*Choose not to give up*
*Never accept defeat*
*We are winners here*

## *Incremental Prosperity*

*Lay weapons down*
*Giving thanks for the people who suffered before*
*you,*
*who are always with you*

*Don't give up*
*We don't give up*

*Let these words give strength*
*Let them motivate*
*Let them inspire*
*Let all that surrounds you be a breath of trust*

*You've always known it*
*They will see the subtle climb you make*
*If you change negative ways*
*Let them doubt you, then impress them,*
*with the god given heartbeat that sounds within*
*you*

*You are doing great*
*Little bit at a time*
*Small moves over time create milestones*
*Do what you can today, be present*
*Wake up tomorrow, do better*

*Take it easy*
*Enjoy the journey*
*Don't lose your senses over it*
*Relax, play*
*Find joy in it*
*Be sensible*

### _Energy In Motion, Emotions_

This world is filled with joy
Don't let the saddened minds influence you
Be the smile spread across the face of all that
comes before you

Should there be times of hardship, know they
will be made soft
Have faith
In the abilities given

To the lives around you, you're just as wonderful
Don't doubt yourself
Don't be hard on yourself, treat yourself with
kindness
You're also deserving

This world is hard enough made of solid ground,
so you're able to walk on it
Walk with, be a friend
Here we can build a safehouse

## *One in the Same*

*In the moments you think you are right*
*You might be*

*Respect the perspective that others have not*
*come to learn*
*For what you have learned is unique to your*
*experience*
*And the experience of others is just the same*
*For this experience gives them a lens you have*
*not faced yourself*

*Mirror Mirror on the wall*
*Who's the _____ of them all*
*No one*
*Everyone*
*In their own way*
*In different eras,*
*Backgrounds*
*Diversification*
*Is not identification*
*Or classification*

*Feel the pulse that beats in you, as it does in*
*others*
*Remember that a thumb print is also a thumbs*
*up*
*For when you point the finger, there's three*
*pointing back*
*And holding up two brings about peace*
*Choose wisely*

## <u>Blueprint Strategy</u>

*Aim to leave people, things, and places better
than you found them
Smile
It's clear
You are here*

*Go about your days with love and gratitude,
for your life and everything surrounding you*

*The tough times have already passed
And all that's going to come is the true beauty of
your essence*

*Have faith*

*You're make belief
It's all good for good
See eyes in kindness*

*Be understanding to the experiences of others
Be forgiving*

*Be proud of the space between your shoulder as
it holds your heart
You are created for a purpose
The purpose is what you make it, but know your
pain is a part of it
Understand the influence
Make it a good one
As you've been made
This is for you
To you
Here reminding you*

*Do good, no harm
Hurting only hurts you and those around you
We love you*

### <u>Beauty Marks</u>

*As you grow you'll make many friends*
*Cherish them like family*
*Some will do you good, others will learn from*
*the kindness in your heart*

*Don't worry*
*Speak kindness not just to others, but yourself as*
*well*
*Choose to be understanding*
*Choose forgiveness*
*Choose stillness*

*Should the dark cover you,*
*look up and see the stars left for you*

*Feel inspired to find heartful treasure*
*For true richness is within the mind and heart,*
*before it is ever found within the hands*
*Smile, you are meant to stay a while*

### Humble Reassurance

A sense of fear might wash over you,
when past decisions have haunted you
Face them
Learn in order to grow and do better
There's miraculous infrastructures and designs,
inventions and creation by others who have used
their talents to mend the pain

Let these moments guide you
Help others learn as well
Stand on your feet
You've been given them for a reason far greater
than just going places

Stand tall and stand firm,
if you know the song that speaks to existence
It's lovely

*Be peaceful*
*Have faith*
*It is not religion,*
*but it can be for those who choose to believe*

*Know that having faith is greater than just this*
*book or anyone else's*
*Place your hand on your heart*
*Feel faith beating*
*-quietly-*
*Understand how it beats in the chest of others*
*Dignity*

## *Character Development*

You're impressive
The way you carry yourself
Care about yourself
It is no burden
Know that you have been carried from the
moment you got here
Helped and loved
Feel the love you've been given over centuries

Take this moment
Close your eyes
See yourself as the child born bringing bliss

Find balance
One step at a time
You are doing the best you can
And with time, you will be able to do better
Success is a process
Don't rush it
It is a thing of beauty when it unfolds
Set intentions
Higher aims
Know what you're shooting for
Alignment
Truthful, heart, mindful experiences

### <u>Big Picture</u>

*There are people that have been deeply hurt by others*
*And maybe you have been one of them*
*I'm sure you have*

*It wasn't easy to grow up with that*
*Love you enough to tell you not to grow in upset*
*But to inspire others to do different*

Heal
Work on yourself
And when you are ready, forgive

Don't rush it
When you are ready

We're here for you
To hear your story
Let the actions you take empower you and those around you

Let go of resentment
The poison
You didn't deserve to drink of
It hinders perception
Fill cups with joy
Nourishment
Love
Empathy

## Lasting Impressions

Share your gifts
Give your presence
Immerse yourself
In things you don't understand
So you and others grow to be understanding

Know the heartbeats created on the side of all
you judge,
matter just as much as you do

Science heals
But know you're the chemistry
Believe and trust your foundation

Trust others to work for you as you have worked
for them
Don't allow a moment of upset to determine the
course of experience

Forgive
Breath and let it go
Grow building others up
Compassion
Perseverance
Resilience

*Just like this book*
*Read many*

*Like the people around you*
*Know that you and them will grow*
*May or may not see tomorrow*
*For even the new dawn brings different weather*

*World full of emotions*
*Challenges and obstacles*
*Embrace change*

*Let the gatherings of homes and community be*
*built by peace*
*You have the right to express yourself*
*Understand the impact*
*Be wise*
*Think thrice!*

## _Healed People, Hear People, Heal People_

Raise your hand on no one with ill intent,
even if it was raised upon you
What have the forms of punishment in the physical,
emotional, verbal, and psychological violence have taught you?

To be scared
To cry
To feel hurt
To walk on eggshells

We are made with minds to process
We learn and teach
Explain yourself
Do it again and again

Delicate minds and hearts
We're sponges, plasticity
The behaviors we inflect can cause deeper harm than imagined
Forming memory imprints
First on ourselves then others
Actions can create a wirement

*Let touch inspire*
*Let it move with grace and gentleness*
*Let it be of love*
*Let it help others rise to do better,*
*by your being better*

*In heightened emotions, take time*
*Separate and distance*
*Know that space is created for that*
*Senses are a blessing*
*No need to numb them*
*Understand inhibitions*
*Fill time with the right distractions*

*Give a helping hand*
*Squash it*
*Talk with care*
*As you've had to feel the hurt of someone else's*
*ways*

*This is just a reminder of your most authentic*
*self*
*Be good to you and those around you*
*It is okay to have made mistakes*
*Today, you are empowered to choose different*
*Compassion*

### _Love_

*Intertwine your hands*
*Breathe deeply*
*Take in this moment to realize,*
*how you have been by your own side*

*That's right!*
*You are your first friend*
*Make that friendship a good one*

*Give yourself moments of clarity*
*A moment for peace*
*A moment of love*
*Appreciation*
*With everything around you and within*
*Here. always have, always will*

## *Joys of Life*

The words of others will guide
Just know how a sweet a new melody sounds
Take in the whole picture
It is anything but one sided
A world made round
Cycles
Make your own path
Feel inspired
It takes courage to walk to discover

These lands were built and founded by those who walked,
not knowing but believing
They too made mistakes
Take a moment to appreciate what has been made of it

A light

Choose to savor the moment
Taste
Sight
Touch
Smell
Listen
To this
Here, now
A Sixth sense

### *Terrain Distinction*

*Legends have passed on leaving you sayings,*
*to get you through the journey*
*Allow yourself to understand them and adopt*
*them*
*Know that what you believe in shapes reality*

*Adopt all that is good*
*The walk of life is not a road*
*It's a playing field*
*That's why it's called a game*
*Don't let the misunderstanding of others,*
*cause you to see worth or the world worse than*
*it really is*

*The time you are living in now is more efficient,*
*more reliable, more safe than it ever has been*
*There are resources*

*The elements are principles*
*At times, pyramids*
*Learn all you can*
*Grow in health and awareness*

## Mi Amor

You are beautiful as you are
With time and change
See more beautiful through a lens of the softest
eyes of acceptance

The true value of beauty shines from within
What's your outlook?
Are you humble to see the beauty between the
lines?
-softer-
The lines that have been written over time,
just like every book speaking the same message
**Love**

They say life is short
Living in the fast lane, it can be
Don't let anyone rush you
Everyone's pace is different

If you doubt this, walk in a park
Know that whether you are young or old,
tall or short,
your strides are proportionately measured to
creation
Be patient
Appreciate the slow pace
Be cautious of how you fuel your tank,
some fluids can stall you
Be aware of consumptions

## <u>Intrinsic Design</u>

Take time to look at strangers and know it is not
a competition
They are part of this family
Deep down, you've known it
The strangers you've met and now call friends
Those that you're born with and have come to
learn from
Good things and bad
Protect your aura
There is beauty in vulnerability
Observe don't absorb it

Aim to not grow bitter
But know it's part of taste buds
What do you like to eat?
Savor the moment
In the movement
Rest
Knowing you will have to climb again
Not over anyone, just thyself

Trust body
Trust mind
Trust
Trust all that is
There is power in we just as much as me

### *Everlasting Union*

Inspiration is encompassed by going north
Rising above
See others as you've come to know yourself
It is bitter
It is sweet
It is a little bit of both
It's a little bit of everything
Just like seasonings
There is seasons
Feel wonderful regardless of the weather

Enjoy the holidays just as others do in different
parts of the world
Happy birthday to you and all those around you
Every day is a celebration
Remember your mission
Speak in truth and honesty
Keep an open mind
Together we'll never fall apart

### *Authenticity from Within*

*After these words*
*Take a moment to feel radiance*

*For just a moment*
*Observe*
*Talk sweetly*
*No one can take that away from you*
*Only you*

*Embrace the seasons with forgiving reason*
*Love*
*Look at those who have helped, hurt, with kindness*
*See them in the beauty as within*

*This world could swallow the best of us but*
*when it spits you out,*
*know it could not hold you down*
*It has made you better*
*Get up*
*Learn*

*Appreciate your surroundings*
*As you are still part of them*
*Without you, the key piece is missing*
*You are the peace made to bring us together*

## Distinct Determination

*Choose health*
*Choose to help*
*Choose to care*
*Choose love*

*Choose to see the good in all that has been designed*
*Inside and outside*

*Lead by example*
*Do not doubt the goodness*
*This space is special*

*Be Brave*
*Have faith*
*No fear*
*Seeded*
*Go with the love that has carried you here*

*Things change*
*Learn to embrace newness*
*And if hardship surrounds you*
*Ask, "What is this trying to teach me?"*
*Lessons are blessings*
*Alchemy*

## Uttered Nourishment

*One step closer to helping each other,*
*singing our song*
*How does your world sound?*
*Go outside*
*Hear it*
*Here it is*
*Learn to love and be the change in it*

*Know the things you do,*
*are a little difference in someone else's life*

*Sustainability*
*Speak politely*
*Manners*
*Rhymes with matter*
*Your ears are closer to the mouth than anyone*
*else*

*Hear you*
*-listen intently-*
*Words create thoughts*
*Speak kindness*
*Not curses of negatives*

## Calligraphy of the Heart

This book is like rose petals to help nourish
Soul enrichment

Read it, pass it on, critique it
This experience is splendid,=
When each grows to embrace it
Not push it away

Learn from it, sweet
And the times it knocks us on our feet
It's meant to slow us down, reminding of why

Values

And know this story is shared with billions
Truth of existence
This time or the next
Seasons of possibilities

## <u>Code of Honor</u>

Challenge yourself to experience something new
That is healthier for you
Meaningful

Take a walk
Dance a little
You can stand there and let it pass you by
But know that taking in the view is just as important as doing the work
Feel accomplished for those "Hello's" given

Your characteristics are the outfit you dress your spirit
How will you speak?
How will you behave?
How will you affect others with the things you say?

Bring to life innovation, creativity, tools as the ones you've come to find
Like the shoelaces that helped protect your feet thus far
This is not a prison
This is heaven on earth
Treat it as good as you treat your favorite places

Home
We share it
Not only amongst our breed
But all life forms
Keep it clean

## *Propelled Elevation*

*Say true*
*To the mission of the soul*
*It might not hum or perfectly rhyme with the world,*
*but you carry your own tune*

*Break barriers but not those around you*
*Just the walls built, to protect you from the hurts*

*Shatter that prison in the mind*
*Play*
*Learn*
*Love*
*Reach higher*

*You will feel grief*
*Harder than the mind can comprehend,*
*but if it helps, know that it's part of the journey*

*Be courageous*
*Be confident*
*Be tolerant*
*Be brave*
*Be smart*
*Be you*

*Keep trying*
*Don't give up*
*Don't ever give up*

# TO YOU FROM YOU

## *Illuminate*

There are special things waiting for you
That will impress you
But for now, take this moment to breathe
Knowing influence matters

You are what the world needs
So get up

Understand that we came before technology
But without innovation we could not live the same
So use precious time to be grateful for it all
Sit around friends and family
Laugh at the day
Share experiences
Share
Input matters
Remember to use manners

*See how others act*
*We're contagious*
*Not diseased*
*There is a deep part of the mind that shifts*
*perception*
*Take your power back*

*Sit outside in a garden or a park*
*For a moment*
*Watch*
*And if you can't see*
*Smell*
*And if you can't smell*
*Touch*
*And if you can't touch*
*Breathe*

## *The Brightside*

*The world is the safest it has been*
*The history of books keep timelines*
*Take a day to read them*
*It's not a battle*
*Its conversations*
*Its disagreements*
*Its temperaments, egos*
*Its empathy, compassion, meetings, and goals*

*So, what will you make of it?*
*Time is precious*

*Full of life*
*Set aside worries for a moment*

*Ah ha!*
*There*
*Crack a smile*

*How awesome is it that?*
*Free medicine*

### *<u>Kinetic Assembly</u>*

*Allow for the uncertainty to be a place of
resources,
healing, and learning
This encouragement is for you
Do with ease*

*When you fail, give yourself credit
It takes guts to be honest
It takes discipline to prioritize
It takes compassion, empathy, and forgiveness to
move past the grief
It requires you to be fully present in all the
emotions meant to feel
Learn to fill your cup*

*When you've mastered that
Help others
Teaching a man to fish can help feed him for a
lifetime
Transfer the energy into a development
A book or structure
Keep growing*

## Social Medicine

Take a moment to see miracles
Witness
Your pain is temporary
Let love in to heal
Moments of happiness shared in collective

Don't let the darkness of one season cloud your
lifetime
Treasure
Bake a cake for a neighbor
Give a gift
Gracious
Give flowers
Give time
Give a moment of silence
Community
Find a way to make a stranger's day
It's not strange

You're an influence
So be the change you wish to see in the world
No matter who is around
No matter who doubts
Be true
Let it start with you
It's within you

## Speaking Into Existence

*The world is your oyster*
*Learn from it what you want*
*Everything in this world serves another*

*Finding a purpose is encompassed within your ability to realize you can do anything you set your mind to*

*Think things through*
*There is more to you than you can possibly imagine*
*The road is open*
*A gift*

*You matter*
*You are loved*
*You are respected*

*Accept age*
*Accept losses*
*Accept sorrow*

*Heal*
*Grow*
*Learn*
*Responsibly*
*Prosperity*

## Heart of Gold

While some inspire you to dream
Others will try to wake you up
While some think you're unconscious
Others will think you're aware

See
Not only in vision
But in all senses of being
Insights

The mystery to life lies within you
You are born into wealth
Never allow the physical world to make you feel
inferior
You are valuable

### *Dancing Star*

*Life might knock you down
But you're not knocked out
Get back in the ring knowing its part of the training
Brush it off your shoulders
Knowing there is so many people who love and support you
Cheering for you*

*Inspire others through grace,
internally knowing you're one moment from feeling a change
Inspire by example
Let passions be the melody of your spirit dancing
Get the basics down and sway within rhythm
Respect the dance of others
As hard and violent as they might swing
It's a learning process
Learn to dodge them
swerve with grace, away from their ways*

### <u>Lean In</u>

Take a moment to pause
Notice what the environment is reflecting back
Words spoken
At times posts, blogs, and articles

Why are thoughts and feelings towards life
different than before?
What is driving it?
Ask questions
The feelings harbored
Where do they stem from?
Where are they rooted?
kindness or disrespect

Journal, keep a diary
See patterns
Research within
You deserve the truth

The creation of innovation was aimed to connect
you
To sooth
Entertain
Educate
Don't abuse it
Understand motivations
Choose to value life than fighting

## <u>Brotherhood</u>

*We lift each other through life from the moment
we're born
All throughout the journey
To the departure of it*

*You have been significant to this place
You have worked at all times of your days
For yourself
For friends
For family
For neighbors
For the planet*

*If you feel down
Trust that it will work for you
We're here to help you*

### *Steadfast*

*Do not give up*
*Don't throw in the towel*
*Take your time*
*For it has been rightfully given to you*
*Take space*
*So see it though*

*The physical body has and will change*
*See in kindness*
*Know it's muscle memory*
*Even behind the eyes*

*Exercise*

*So you are able to let go of the toxicity that*
*exhausts you*
*Nurture*
*There is only one of you*

*How do you feel?*
*Are you happy?*
*Are you sad?*
*Are you numb?*
*Are you alive?*

*Life, is this moment*
*So don't run from it*

*Even with every obstacle*
*You will get stronger*
*No one learned to ride a horse before falling off*
*its back*
*Your pitfall is anything from rock bottom*
*Slingshot forward*

### *Vital Vision*

Take a moment to stand completely still in a city
Watch with your eyes
Hear with your ears
Smell with your nose
Feel with your senses, priceless moments
As you breath in all the miracles that surround
you
People all around
The particles of dust

You share something so special with everything
that is life
You are part of this story
A belonging
Treasured

## _Respectful Civilization_

A mission statement is part of every organiza-
tion that has succeeded
Understand that your mission creates an
influence,
in your life and millions of others

Let intentions be of good and not of greed
Let it be something that honors the people,
that have helped you get here

Let it be something you want to be apart of,
from the inside and out
Treat those that work with you,
never for you, with respect

It is in the numbers of the souls you nurture,
that determines your richness

They've always said don't bite more than you
can chew
How much can you consume?
Share with those around you
Learn for yourself, then teach another

### *Value of Richness*

The little things that you do are a big deal
Feel inspired to choose different
You've been given limbs and an intellect to strive
It's all in strides, baby steps
Do all things with care

Some elements will catch you by surprise
A redirection
Practice of virtues

As things become clear and fog clears
Get strong
Then get up
Feed your life, then feed another

### <u>Universal Welfare</u>

*Chaos is a place in the mind,
displaced by chemicals of poison and pain,
loss and grief
At times, it's because others don't believe
Of all the goodness that resides here,
because of all they had experienced*

*Just know you are loved
Your life matters and have been saved all along*

*Some may find you at your best and leave you
at your worst
Be patient through
As impulsive as it is to react in negativity
Learn the magnetitic field*

*There will be those who pick you up and hold
you
Giving free gifts
Also whispering reassurance*

*These people matter
We all have them
We will lose them
We will find them again
And we will become them*

### *Bullseye*

*Keep having faith
No matter the tides*

*There are secrets in this world that you won't
find the answers to written in plain sight
They're felt with the heart
Patterns
Trust its all for a purpose
Embrace*

### *Resonance*

*Use knowledge to power*
*Knowing you don't know everything*

*Use and build talents and skills*
*Relax*
*Smile*

*Facial expressions are impressions of time*
*They have been shared through timelines*
*Empathy*
*Forgive*
*So easy and quick when needed*

## Inquisitive Inquiries

*You are here, still*
*So what does that mean to you?*
*I hope you can learn to be different and the same*
*In the ways that help*

*Know that you have been part of many wishes*
*See how your mannerisms are of those that have*
*been with you and around you*
*Use this to enlighten you*

## Structural Composition

*It won't make sense when it is unfolding because*
*your brain is designed to protect you*
*Feel what you need, then release*

Trust instincts
Be cautious of impulses
Understand the difference
At the balance of reason
Calculating the next step is significant

What will you make of it?
Time is on your side
Manage it
Spend it
Where focus go, energy follows
Currency
Electric

## <u>Peace Within</u>

*This page was white before these words were written*
*Just like actions taken*

*What kind of impact do you want to make?*
*After reading this, I hope you learn to leave a beauty mark*

*Authenticity*
*Accountability*
*Love*
*Empathy*
*Compassion*
*Humility*
*Gratitude*
*Wellness*
*A story of becoming*
*True essence*

## Gratitude

Here you find all you could ever want
Just keep in mind what you're yearning for
Understand motivations, needs,
aspirations, and fears

What can be used or leveraged?
Marketing
Targets
Vulnerabilities which may be exploited
Grow awareness


How do you feel?
Are you craving more?
Give thanks
Sometimes all it takes is a little change
Appreciation
Love
Helping hands
Striving in all aspects of design
Here, now
Even in the silence of the mind

### *<u>Harmony of Choice</u>*

*How much do you fill in your cart?
If you saw all those things as canvases in a
museum,
would you walk in it?
Expression in utterance*

*They often say less means more
But look all around you and inside of you
There is nothing small about you*

*In the beauty of designed
This world can never define or encompass
Soulful radiant us*

*You have the power to be anything you wanted
It is all within you
Don't let others cloud you*

## Compounded Momentum

As you've grown to learn one skill after the next
From standing on your feet
To giving a helping hand
Building and constructing
With a song
or a smile
Words of embrace,
left in this space

Leave the past behind
Know what it has taught you

All you stand upon came from the support of
those before you
See true beauty
Why hate?

-be still-

You are safe
Strong
Beautiful
Lead with dignity and respect
Honorable

### Answer to You

*Pain is a sweet sensor*
*Listen to the signals*

*Know there is a genius in you,*
*no one but you is able to figure out*
*And some might find a way to relate to it*
*Or hinder it*
*Cheer it on*
*Or belittle it*

*But let the little things move you*
*Bit by bit*
*Breathe it in*
*Insight*
*What do you see?*

*Look within*
*You hold a key*
*Get curious*

### Neo-Cortex

If you're moving fast,
the frames of your surroundings pass you by
Like you're watching out of the window of a car
And if you're high, it's a plane sight

So I ask you
What do you see?
How do you feel?
Did you wake up to see the sun
If not, did you feel the wind?
If not, did you talk to a loved one?
If not, did you stretch
If not, did you drink some water?

Feel how we've come already whole
Gratitude
Pour in your cup value

## *Revival*

*On the worst days*
*And on the best*
*Give thanks*

*Even the most terrible of situations can be a*
*silver lining*
*Accept things for the lessons they bring*

*Reflections*
*Evaluations*

*There are beautiful things here*
*Feel the beauty of soul radiance*
*Even unseen*

*Give into humanity*
*That of strength and that of weakness*
*That of love and that of pain*

*Life*
*It decays*
*It's okay*

## <u>Life</u>

Here in these pages, you'll find friends and
family
Science of man
Engineered on
Started on the walls of stone
And continues to evolve

But you are chemistry,
beyond words or understanding

Stay true and honest
With yourself most importantly
It serves the source of all that's around you

## <u>United Nations</u>

We often hold truths,
from the experiences we've had and eventually
thrive to share

Your parents tried their best
Forgive them
If they're here, still with you, love them
If you hold onto a child, bear them
Like a little teddy bear given as sentiment of the
love that binds us

The best of is in the rest
Some have come to learn
Some have never been exposed to the challenges
A world is a playground
Full of obstacles
It is a home in which you walk through

Help someone who's lost their way
Whether it be a neighbor across the street or
countries away
We're in it together
Don't give up on them
See yourself within them
Heartbeat rhythm

### Human Race

The experience is unique
Feel inspired
Learn to share and grow in ways that serve
Don't compare progress

Focus
Stay in your lane
Don't crash into anyone else
But know accidents happen,
know co-incidence

Remember to celebrate little wins
Success
No accident
Earned
As it is for others
Not getting first, gets you second
We're never losers
Understand the race in being human
From all walks with through life

## <u>Ripple Effect</u>

Smile
Hug
Visit a playground
See yourself in those children playing there
What legacy do you want to share?
How do you build and pave the way?
Reflect on behaviors and actions

Be leaders and followers
Teachers and students
Different ages and generations
One ceases to exist without the other
Get along
Get with it

Bet on the future
You're part of it
Moment after moment as it passes by
Don't be intimated to step into your light
The stage is yours
The sun shines on all of us
Rooting for you

## *Principle Bound*

Take a moment to breathe
Here you are
Now
All the mountains you've climbed

Ah! Here you are!

As you hold this written
From a source they call spirit
A guidance
Inner truth
Don't give up on you
Always have faith
Trust authentically like your life dependent on it
It sometimes does

Do good
Even if you're misunderstood
Take care of the body
Nourish the soul
Understand what's feeding you
Life nurtures

Embrace change
You're a warrior
Not a worrier
Creative prime

### <u>Nobel Duty</u>

*See the journey through
Pain of loss, hurt, grief,
and destruction may be present
But I ask to bring fresh ideas,
actions, and words to help build life for the better*

*Heal it
Nurture it
Pluck out the weeds
Take a moment
Learn focus
Solitude
Lean in
Not against
We're created equal even within abilities*

*Empower those that need to be reminded,*
*of their true beauty, even with their scars*
*True strength*
*Talents within the limitations*

*We come here not knowing*
*Develop meaning*
*Look at life as learning opportunities*
*Lessons and blessings*

*This perspective will move you*
*Ready to see you*
*Alongside those who helped you*
*For they have come before, with, and after you*

*Rise friend, rise*
*You can be one of the legends*
*Feel inspired to give life, lifeful gifts*
*Through your existence*

### Gracious Heart

Have you drank a glass of water when thirsty?
That quench
That "Ah... this is all I needed"
In this moment,
drink up from the well
Grow feeling inspired

Take time
It's alright dear one,
you're okay

Feel comforted
Give and receive love, beloved

This is within
The process takes time
Know time is on your side
Don't throw the opportunity
Show up
For others, as well as yourself
It does get better

## *Honey Do*

See past your enemies to their truth
They're people too
Don't let the uniform separate you
Honor and respect

The frustrations we carry are not against the
eyes before us
The ideas, opinions, and perspectives of things
that no longer serving us

Purify the hatred and resentments felt
First within yourself

Focus on creating joy
It won't be easy
It'll be worth it
For what is felt by you will be felt amongst the
rest

Be patient
Virtuous
Developing the planet better
Don't be bitter
Pick up your litter

## *Splendid Reassurance*

*We are born to share the classroom with others*
*It is not just about the self*
*Feel compassion for the new*
*Be brave, teaching "Hello's"*

*There is another reading this as well*
*In the most unexpected ways*
*Change tides*

*How lucky am I?*
*When was the last time you thought that to yourself?*
*Challenge you to speak it outloud*
*And see what will be made of it*
*New vision*

## *Radiance*

*We're here to help*
*To make it blossom*

*The little parts of this make up*
*Hearts that oxygenate the vessels*
*The limbs and muscles*
*Nerve Fibers*

*Applying foundations*

## <u>Regenerative</u>

Get back in the playground
You might eat a different lunch
You might not jump as high
You might not see it all the same
It might feel different
Reminiscing of time passed

Just breathe
If you can breathe
You're still here
And if you're still here, there is more great things
waiting for you
Feel the breeze

Feel the sunshine in the winter day as it warms
up your skin
Whatever you do, however you do it
Keep going and growing

Even to the afterlife
Let the spirit embrace change
Open the heart again
Love
Do improvingly different

## Dreamers Awake

*Gently understand*
*And know what handprints and footprints were*
*left within*

*Define your qualities*
*Practice them*
*Build your character*

*Life will knock you down*
*Sometimes you could slip from your own doing*
*Other times from not knowing*
*But just like your first steps,*
*learn to pick yourself up again*

*Don't stress it*

*You are here to love and be loved, beloved*
*To experience beautiful things*

*Put in the work*
*For it lays the foundation of your experience and*
*that of others*
*Follow your passions*
*But take time to understand the heat that fuels*
*them*
*Motivations*
*Linguistics*
*Understand language*

## <u>Destiny</u>

*If it has not gone your way, breathe deeply*
*Knowing that the most beautiful things have*
*been in the works for you*

*This breath you have is a great gift*
*Accept circumstances and learn to move and*
*acquire again*
*There is plenty for everyone*
*And if you ever feel shattered or broken*
*Please, hold on*
*Be gentle*
*Take time*

*Do not doubt the strength*
*Do not doubt the magic*
*The science*
*The creation, you have been made of*
*Sensible*
*Don't lose your senses*

*Continue learning*
*Reason,*
*"What is this trying to teach me?"*

## <u>Cognitive Dissonance</u>

There are challenges along the route
At times it might feel like an obstacle course
Other times a circus or a crisis
It is going to be okay

If you've gotten injured
Tend to your wounds
Heal

Cherish the little things
They will be the big things as the clock winds down

Utilize the environment for care
Not harm
Just because it's there, don't feel enticed to participate

### *Savor*

*Some say to count your blessings*
*First, I ask you to simply breathe*
*With each breathe*
*Relax*

*Feel the body working to keep you alive without*
*conscious effort*
*How great is that?*
*Appreciate it*
*Understand what fuels it*

*Understand doings*
*Habits*
*Remember to be*
*And learn of your being*
*From human beings*
*There is more to the eye than one can perceive*
*Manifests*

### *Let It In*

*Sit outside if you could watch for a moment*
*As everyone works like the little cells in your*
*body to make sure it's functioning*
*Reorganize as needed*
*Don't rush it*
*Be patient*
*Wounds take time to heal*
*And at times they may scar*

*In some cases, you may lose something you can't*
*replace*
*Pain is a tear*
*Hurt heart*
*Tread light*

*Trust to let it go understanding what you lose*
*never really goes away*
*Because love is on its way*

*Let tears stream*
*But don't dwell long*
*Grieve*
*Feel it through*

*And when you're ready to use that pain for good*
*Transform it in a way that helps*
*There are eyes to meet and hands to shake*
*Here to help grow soul enrichment*

### <u>Supernova</u>

The science of the journey speaks for itself
Let intentions, in good conscious, help and heal

It is okay to love
And it is okay to hurt
Know that it takes time to feel both

Don't brace for the worst
Embrace all that is
Change
Keep a positive attitude
Even if it doesn't make sense
Trust senses and instincts

Remember who you are
Where you've been
Take care darling
This is lifting you higher

## *Way of the World*

*As you listen to the stories of others,
exercise empathy and gentleness
Share stories so it could put things in perspective
Thinking is a utility
Don't misuse memory while embracing honesty*

*See things as they are and how they could be
better
Feel inspired
The believers are the ones that change the world
Don't be scared
Even with any mistakes you might have made
Seek forgiveness*

*Believe in the truth of people
Experiences are real
Don't be desensitized
We collaborate
We hold unions
United, friends, and neighbors
Respect
And love
Foundation of a collective*

### <u>Happy Birthday</u>

This is just the beginning
And if it feels like the end
Don't you think it truly has been a great one?

Stay hopeful and driven
Persevere in all your endeavors

Learn for yourself or learn from another
Grow to understand the lessons as they become
blessings

Take care of yourself and those around you

*Thank you*

## About the Author

Farah Alqattan was born in 1989, in a small country known as Kuwait. At a young age, she was able to develop a strong sense of resiliency and grit. Farah spent the first 7 years of her childhood adventuring in a collective society while being conditioned on values of kindness and peace through Islam.

In January of 2000, the American Dream came to fruition when Farah along with her family migrated to the United States. Having little financial means, intellectual knowledge, and support, Farah and her family were helped by strangers, teachers, public servants, and public officers.

After coming out in 2012, Farah sought to develop her independence. She felt her values and that of her culture misaligned. And just like that, she was off to adventures.

On September 13, 2019 Farah deeply reflected on her circumstances in life and decided to make a shift while starting to meditate. She pondered the statement made by JFK "Ask not what your country can do for you; ask what you can do for your country." Shortly after, during the COVID pandemic of 2020, her highest calling came through in creativity and inspiration spurring "To you From you". Her story has had a whirlwind of emotions that significantly affected her. After some time, she was able to connect the dots on many of her experiences while writing this book. And like a planted flower in a garden, so has been her story.

Farah now blooms working within the field of cybersecurity. She's inspired to speak and share her story to bridge perspective on diverse upbringings. Farah is known to be philosophical and intellectual and those closest to her see the depth of her passion and care for humanity and nature.

www.farahalqattan.com

## About the Publisher

Rwh Publishing LLC was established in 2023 to publish creative content by artists that aim to uplift humanity and change lives for the better.

A portion of the proceeds from this book will be utilized to developing an infrastructure the aids individuals to feel grounded and centered, contributing to mind, body, and soul alignment along with strengthened character development.

Thank you for your support!

*"For where your treasure is, there your heart will be also"*

### Up Next!

*Oh, did we mention there's more!?*

Subscribe to author notifications, by visiting **www.farahalqattan.com**, and be the first to preorder next book in the series. Promo code **HaveHope** for an exclusive 15% discount.

www.ingramcontent.com/pod-product-compliance
Lightning Source LLC
Chambersburg PA
CBHW020333010526
44119CB00002B/49